PREHAB

PREHAB

Leveraging Perception to End Substance Abuse

Patrick N. Moore LPC

Duncan Park Press LLC
Atlanta

Published by Duncan Park Press LLC, 4554 Mansell Road, Suite 300, Alpharetta, GA 30022; 770-521-4212

Prehab © 2016 Duncan Park Press LLC All rights reserved.

ISBN 978-0-9979670-0-5

ISBN 978-0-9979670-1-2 ebook

Library of Congress Control Number: 2016920181

Printed in the United States of America

First edition

Second printing 2017

This book contains information about risk related to Substance Use Disorders in terms of perception, behavior, outcomes and severity for educational purposes. The models and assessments in this book are not intended to replace Medical or Mental Health Professionals. For any questions or choices regarding your health or someone else's contact your local medical or mental health facility. For any emergencies call 911. The Author and Publisher disclaim responsibility for any adverse effects resulting directly or indirectly from information contained in this book.

Permission to use "Eagles Fan" for Commitment example granted by John R. DePaul

Author photo courtesy of Amanda Lively

CONTENTS

Student Comments   vii

Dedication Page   ix

Final Title Page   xi

Quote page   xiii

Preface   xv

Acknowledgements   xix

1. Introduction   1
2. The Cause   7
3. Experimenting With Perception   11
4. Defeating the Prevention Paradox   17
5. Risk / Benefit and Other Perception Risk Factors   23
6. How Perception Works   27
7. The MAPP Model   45
8. Find Your Risk Level and Understand Theirs   59

9. Low Benefit Perception Problem   69

10. Perception is High Benefit   75
    Leverage

11. Recovery MAPP   81

12. How to End It   93

About the Author   106

Appendix I Fear Sheet   109

References   111

STUDENT COMMENTS

Thank you for being so informative, I'm going to change some of my habits.

It's interesting to know that most people who are harmed by Alcohol are those that are not necessarily addicted.

You helped me understand me ten times better and the risks I am at. Thank you for helping me out.

I have had a family member at stage 4 and this presentation helped me understand what he is / was going through.

All freshmen must know this information about addictions.

Lecture was helpful on understanding the evolutionary reason behind addiction. How the brain works.

———————

This helped me open my eyes to see the truth about alcohol and drug use / abuse. Thank you so much for taking the time to teach me, and help me become aware of the effects and the future effects this usage withholds.

———————

The 4 stages really helped me realize that I may have a bigger problem than I thought + I could really relate to a lot of the mental processes described in the addiction cycle.

———————

This presentation opened my eyes. I like the speaker's use of personal experience.

———————

Very good presentation. I hope that all learning communities see this presentation.

———————

The instructor for this course did the impossible, he made a drug and alcohol awareness class interesting

To Donna, with love, just the way you are.

In loving memory of Raynor and Tweetie

PREHAB
Leveraging Perception to End Substance Abuse

...we are not just an amygdala and a puddle of stress hormones. We do have some pretty powerful abilities to think, to analyze, and to reason *(Ropeik, 2010, p. 215-216).*

PREFACE

…the automatic System 1 is the hero of the book *(Kahneman,
2011, Chapter 1, Section 1, para. 3).*

Sanctioned research and professional groups are guided by ethics. Most everyone is familiar with do no harm – also known as non-malfeasance. This ethic in and of itself is good, but not good enough.

The work in this book involves two other ethics: autonomy and beneficence. Autonomy is the desired result for clients and what this book is about.

Doing good – beneficence – is necessary to avoid wasting time or misleading the client. In order to claim good requires a measurement, also what this book is about.

As coordinator for Alcohol and Other Drug (AOD) education at Kennesaw State University (KSU) prior attempts at measuring AOD education outcomes had failed for us and many others. So much so it was stated in a respected publication (Babor et al., 2010, p. 216) "It is likely that even with adequate resources, strategies that try to use education to prevent alcohol-related harm are unlikely to deliver large or sustained benefits."

The evidence is on Babor's side. Failures are informative. Does this mean education does not work?

Material progress in the last 50 years related to psychology, physics, computing, engineering, communication and many other measures suggests education works very well. More likely it is time for AOD education to catch up with recent research and discoveries.

The determination to measure outcomes created a new strategy that was to some degree already in place. Continued application and integration of models from treatment, perception research, risk communication, personality development and individual psychology opened new doors.

I did not anticipate the following: new models need new assessments; new assessments yield new data; new data requires analysis, new analysis leads to new conclusions, more models and measurements.

This cycle stopped when it was discovered that perception is the problem, solution and leverage for change. Kahneman was right. System 1 is the hero. Stumbling across a way to measure this process felt like capturing lightening in a bottle.

> Given student responses and reduced negative consequences, the human affective response system can be developed through education.

The implications reach far beyond the narrow scope of alcohol-related harm to an autonomous defense against all harms.

Prehab is the latest design of those discoveries. We (students, faculty and staff) had fun and enjoyed the privilege of relaying useful, relatable, effective information. My hope is that same energy can be passed on in book form so others may leverage perception and discover insights about themselves or someone they care about.

I believe, armed with these simple facts, the coming generation can experience development faster to a greater degree.

Waiting to see who lives, dies or responds to treatment are no longer the only options.

December 19, 2016
Patrick N. Moore LPC
4555 Mansell Rd. Suite 300
Alpharetta, GA 30022

ACKNOWLEDGEMENTS

Family and friends are everything. I thank them all—past and present, especially anyone who endured me over the last five years. Your patience, love and interest meant more than you know.

My son's awareness of order and my daughter's determination to contribute is visible in all parts of our families and reflected in this book. Thank you for sharing your gifts with each other and the world.

Thanks to my brother Carl and family for listening and consulting. I thank the writers in the family, Anne Moore, Psy.D. and Elizabeth DePaul, Ph.D. for their example and inspiration.

Thanks to Teresa Johnston, MA, LPC and the Center for Young Adult Addiction and Recovery (CYAAR) and the following departments and committed staff at Kennesaw State University (KSU) for the courage to try something new to benefit students: Student Conduct and Academic Integrity, First Year Programs, Greek life, Department of Athletics, Counseling and Psychological Services, Melissa Lewis in the early days, the Center for Health Promotion and Wellness, and Mr. Carol Dwight Perry for sharing his time and experience. A special thank you to the peer educators and student participants. Go Owls.

As a counselor I belong to a family of theorists and practitioners starting with Alfred Adler. Other influences compatible with Adler include Myers (1995), Gardner (2008), Kahneman (2011) and Ropeik (2010). These in turn led to education, psychology and communication resources that include: Ambrose et al. (2010), Burns (2010), Frank & Frank (1991), Manaster & Corsini (1982), Sandman (2009), Miller & Rollnick (2002), Smagorinsky, Cook & Johnson (2003), Bazerman & Tenbrunsel (2011), Brafman & Brafman (2008), Diamond (2013), Richards (2012) and Morgan et al. (2002).

I stand on the shoulders of the following researchers: Myers & Myers (1995), Schinke,

Botvin, Orlandi (1991), Frank & Frank (1991), Miller & Sanchez (Howard & Nathan, 1994), Babor et. al (2010), Cummings (2001), McLeod (2003) and Babbie (2004).

I wish to thank some of the individuals who encouraged or spent time to listen: Brad Hieger, Ph.D.; Sue Swanson, PhD; Leanne Henry-Miller LPC; John Gano; Bill Head; Sam Russell; Steve Smigelski; Matt Erwin, CACII; Robert Bell; Evan Scheffer; Wes Johnson; Tim Hansen CAC I; Julie Hansen, Ph.D.; Liz Lang; Michael Polacek B.S.; Lindsay Montgomery; Jessica McDaniel; Dr. Larry Jedlicka, MD, Ph.D.; Tom Palazzo; Ewell Hardman, M.Div., MAC, CCS; Donald Gregg, Ed.D., LPC, CPCS; David Blackwell, Ed.S.; Jody Housker, Ph.D., LPC; and GSAP members. There are more, forgive me if I did not mention you.

Finally, thanks to Michelle Watson for editing and asking the right questions and the talented Bryan Reed for the cover design.

CHAPTER 1

INTRODUCTION

Man will become better when you show him what he is like.- *Anton Chekhov*

P rehab is a presentation of models that recognize and solve the basic human dilemma best described by an individual psychology concept: humans are brilliant perceivers but not always good interpreters. From an evolutionary psychology perspective this is no accident. As Pinker (2002) points out, we are not blank slates. Humans are born pre-equipped. Modeling the process of this affective response system presents choices that directly affect development of our gifts. The process begins with survival.

The contest for dominance between logic and feeling was decided in caveman days. In an environment where hesitation meant extinction, feeling – also called affect – won. As Kahneman suggests in chapter one (2011) thinking fast is good, but not without fault and bias. This explains a paradox. Humans are rational; evidence suggests we live and die by affect. This is a development problem.

This is the cost of survival; perception comes first, judgment later. These concepts are more than interesting theory. They are more than methods to create wealth or outrage. They are applicable to one of our most persistent and damaging public health challenges, substance use disorders.

The Motivational Assessment Prevention Program (MAPP) model utilizes the factors driving affect into an assessment. The MAPP model and assessment are designed to explain direction and magnitude of risk in terms of behavior, perception and outcome, based on personal experience, not someone else's interpretation.

The perception-driven and judgment-based models uses the MAPP assessment for development. Dependence is illustrated in the perception-driven model. The judgment-based model leverages perception risk factors in terms of risk and benefit. The result is development. When perception serves judgment, the affective response system becomes the solution instead of the problem.

Without this understanding humans are faced with the cruel challenge of correcting something they don't really understand.

This is not a book about the danger of drugs, how to behave, increasing risk perception, treating symptoms, or unsupported theories of addiction and treatment. Prehab is not promoting intervention based on indication, that's Rehab.

Prehab is the missing educational intervention necessary for a paradigm shift in reducing negative outcomes related to acute consequences and unwanted habituation. Evidence from this research suggests learning is contagious; it spreads.

When students anonymously self-assess on an accurate model, understanding and learning are the products. This aids the Vygostkian "twisting path" of learning scientific concepts as so well described by Smagorinsky, Cook & Johnson (2003). Learning is change.

A paradigm shift may sound preposterous unless, like every other worthy outcome, realistic objectives and goals are planned and executed. Recent research made the following objectives and plan possible.

OBJECTIVES

1. Isolate and research use disorder causes.
   Fear. Perception. The prevention paradox.
2. Reverse engineer perception related to substance use disorders.
   Risk / benefit and other risk perception factors.
3. Integrate perception and behavior in a

measurable, progressive model.
Assess your direction and magnitude of
 risk or anyone else's.
4. Illustrate perception leverage by risk
 and benefit.
 How perception serves rather than
 replaces judgment.
5. Codify how to end substance use
 disorders.
 Continuum-based collaboration and
 intervention.

PLAN

The primary Prehab goal is
autonomy—freedom from external control or
influence – combined with the efficacy
required to achieve the goal.

    The strategy is continuum-based
intervention. The primary objective is
accurately self assessing direction and
magnitude of all risk levels in terms of
perception and judgment. Effectiveness is
increased through collaboration in the
community. Logistical research challenges
like treatment fidelity, and attrition are solved

by integrating models and assessment over time in one presentation.

The next 11 chapters introduce the rationale, research and working parts of this plan for implementation at the level of individuals, groups or cultures.

Humans are too smart to be rational at all times. Embracing this perspective—without fear and bias—paves a path to autonomy, the opposite of dependence.

If enough of the right people understand causality and what to do about it, addiction can be retired as a relic of a bygone era. There is suffering enough; the time for ending needless suffering is at hand.

Chapter 2

THE CAUSE

The great enemy of the truth is very often not the lie – deliberate, contrived, dishonest – but the myth, persistent, persuasive and unrealistic. Too often we hold fast to the clichés of our forbears. We subject all facts to a prefabricated set of interpretations. We enjoy the comfort of an opinion without the discomfort of thought. *John F. Kennedy (Schlesinger, 1965, p. 238) as seen in Chickering and Reisser (1993, p. 459)*

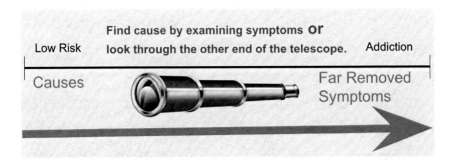

M yths related to far removed symptoms to explain addiction must go. Results and outcomes in Severe Use Disorders are stark and traumatic. They are not causes.

Drugs or drug-like processes, are necessary for use disorders: they are not sufficient. Most people can drink, shop, gamble, eat, or have sex without experiencing a use disorder.

Loneliness, anti-social behavior, cross addiction or any other kind of demoralization are results. Results from habituating a perception driven process.

Underlying any dysfunctional outcome is either too much or too little fear. Fear is a perception process. A perception-driven process over time is the cause of any use disorder. The working parts of this process are called perception risk factors (Ropeik, 2010, p. 67). For better or worse, these risk factors drive our affective risk response systems.

The same risk factors can generate courage. Courage is a judgment process. A judgment-based process over time prevents any use disorder. The difference between process driven and judgement based is how and when risk factors are used.

Never before have we known more about why we do the things we do. The mystery has been taken out of the affective risk response system. How we balance risk and benefit in a given circumstance is known. Armed with these facts, the models in this book allow anyone to know exactly how perception-driven or judgment-based they were, are, and will be.

Educational intervention changes risk-perception factors from inevitable agents of self-destruction to generators of good not yet imagined. These conclusions are based on the application of the latest perception theory.

The next section is a summary of the research that inspired this book and how to defeat the primary barrier to real change.

CHAPTER 3

EXPERIMENTING WITH PERCEPTION

However, a serious deficit of type development, especially a deficit of judgment, constitutes a disability for which no amount of intelligence can compensate (*Myers, 1995, p. 177*).

Few have contributed more than Isabel Myers to understanding perception and judgment for the purposes of development.

Research has uncovered another layer of perception beneath a sensing / intuition model. The prehab model extends Myer's application of Jungian concepts to personal development related to risk and substance use disorders.

The following is a brief overview of the

correlations discovered through research on a college campus.

Nonequivalent measures were used to compare risk levels in this college population.

In the fall of 2014 in a convenient freshman college sample, n=457, a high correlation was found (r = .999996) between MAPP risk categories and risk levels published by the World Health Organization (Babor, Higgins-Biddle, 2001, p. 33).

During Spring and Fall semesters of 2014, 923 college students participated in the prehab presentation and MAPP assessment at Kennesaw State University.

Depending on the pattern of the assessment response, students were classified into risk categories now called perception-driven, judgment-based or moving from perception driven to judgment based. Increased judgment categories correlate with reduced negative consequences on campus.

The outcomes of the assessments and negative consequences for 2014 are illustrated in Tables 1 and 2.

Table 1

Perception-Driven (PD) and Judgment-Based (JB) Results

2014	n=923		
JB	PD	PD to JB	Total JB
54.92%	15.52%	29.56%	84.48%

Table 2

Combined Disciplinary Actions – On-campus Student Housing Facilities U.S. Department of Education Campus Safety and Security http://ope.ed.gov/campussafety/#/customdata/search

	KSU	GA Southern	UGA	GA Tech	GA State
2013	408	290	196	127	190
2014	367	443	228	169	309
% decrease	10.0	-52.8	-16.3	-33.0	-62.6

The results in Table 1 indicate 29.56% of this student sample moved from perception-driven (PD) to judgment-based (JB) after the presentation and assessment.

As seen in Table 2, Negative outcomes decreased by ⟨10⟩ percent at KSU as measured by the Department of Education.

KSU was the only school compared to four similar public universities to decrease negative outcomes from 2013 to 2014.

Continued studies, discussion, and analysis yielded the following conclusions:

- The student is the smartest person in the room.

- Use disorder risk = hazard x exposure x affective response system development.

- Prehab education is a catalyst for affective response system development.

- The low risk are most at risk (prevention paradox).

- Continuum-based objectives defeat the prevention paradox.

- Continuum-based collaboration develops a judgment-based culture.

- The cause of use disorders is a perception-driven process over time.

No research is perfect; no lab can control all

variables. The advance in this research is the discovery of a measurable education method to encourage development anywhere on the risk continuum. If education is useful, outcomes will be different. Given the evidence, the prehab intervention is not only statistically significant, but practically important and clinically significant (McLeod, 2003, p. 134).

An updated model of causality helps, but not enough to overcome the primary barrier to progress.

Success in decreasing negative consequences related to use disorders is directly related to the degree the prevention paradox is allowed to exist.

CHAPTER 4

DEFEATING THE PREVENTION PARADOX

If we cure every case of addiction in this country, nothing would change. *-Stephen O'Neil at the 2013 Georgia School of Addiction Conference during his SBIRT presentation.*

The Prevention Paradox
Research has "found that the majority of acute alcohol problems occurred among the majority of drinkers with low or moderate risk". (Babor et al. 2010 p.69)

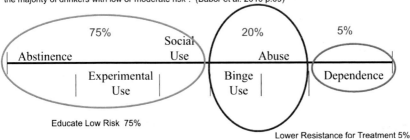

(Used with permission of Stephen O'Neil, 2012)

ost accidents and premature deaths happen to the majority of users at low to moderate risk, not the high-risk minority (Babor et al., 2010, p. 69; Kreitman, 1986; Rose, 1981, p. 1847-51; Spurling & Vinson, 2005). These are the circumstances of the prevention paradox. In spite of enormous investment and success, negative acute and chronic consequences continue. The statistics are alarming when tobacco (450,000 annual fatalities) is combined with all other drugs. War pales in comparison to what we do to ourselves.

> The total annual damage in the U.S.A. directly related to dependence disorders is 500,000 addiction related deaths, costing US Citizens hundreds of Billions of dollars (*Barlow & Durand, 2005, p. 379*).

The solution seems obvious—stop focusing on the chronic end of the continuum and start focusing on the whole continuum of risk. This is much easier said than done.

One underlying issue is measurement. It's hard to let go of a yardstick everyone agrees on.

All evidenced-based interventions are based on behaviors. Behaviors like quantity, frequency and consequences are measurable. These measurements are categorized. The categories indicate levels of risk and corresponding levels of treatment. Less behavior is evidence of a successful intervention.

Meanwhile the wreckage continues for the low risk, un-indicated, un-screened and misdiagnosed. Something has to change.

A similar challenge was solved in WWII as illustrated by Livio, (2013, Chapter 11, Section 3, para. 6). Planes and personnel returning to England from their missions over Europe were badly damaged and shot up. A team was formed to study these planes.

Their objective was to isolate where damage was most likely to occur so that extra armor could be installed to increase protection of the plane and crew.

The final report (Abraham Wald's recommendation) of this study was unexpected but accurate. Put the armor where there are no holes.

It was explained that all of the planes studied, no matter how shot up, made it back. To Wald, the planes that did not return had holes elsewhere, or they would have made it back.

The tendency to focus on the planes that made it back is called selection bias, a distortion caused by data-collecting tools or methods.

When disease and outcomes are overemphasized a selection bias occurs. The lower risk are ignored—or worse, treated ineffectively. This explains the inverse relationship between positive empirical results by evidence based treatment and poor results in the population.

Without knowing it at the time, the decision to target all risk levels at KSU nullified the prevention paradox and selection bias.

The myth that intervening on the indicated is necessary and sufficient must be destroyed before it destroys us more than it already has.

Rather than the focus, addiction became what it is: the unintended progressive consequence of a perception-driven process over time. Freedom to examine the continuum for more than behavior made interventions at all risk levels possible.

Rather than waiting for progression to indicate a problem, continuum based education intervenes on progression itself.

Neither Moderate nor Severe Use Disorders can exist in the absence of progression. Over time defeating the prevention paradox inevitably defeats addiction.

An understanding of how people perceive risks and benefits makes a developmental risk assessment possible.

An accurate risk level begins the process of moving from perception-driven to judgment-based by choice.

CHAPTER 5

RISK / BENEFIT AND OTHER PERCEPTION RISK FACTORS

Better understanding cannot guarantee changes in behavior; those depend on how people perceive benefits as well as risks, and on their resources and constraints *(Morgan et al., 2002, p. 14)*.

Communicating risk is informative. If change or autonomy is the goal communication must tap the realm of the psychological. Behavioral economics and cognitive behavioral interventions take into account both risk and benefit and how either is influenced by perception. Similar insights can be applied to the Substance Use Disorder continuum.

The building blocks that influence perception are masterfully illustrated in *The*

Science of Fear by Daniel Gardner. The titans of perception research are reported on in an interesting manner. For example, Slovic and Alhakami are cited for research demonstrating the see saw relationship between good / bad and risk / benefit (Gardner, 2008, p. 71). These examples of affect bias are called perception risk factors in Ropeik (2010) and the MAPP model.

Risk / benefit is the key risk factor in the MAPP model. There are many other risk factors. They all impact our perception of risk and benefit. They all operate on the following principles (2010, p. 68) as described by Ropeik:

- Each factor can increase or decrease fear.

- Factors can combine increasing their power.

- Biases and other inputs can combine and increase power.

- Risk perception factors are universal.

The question becomes which risk factors in

what order affect which parts of the risk continuum?

Treatment and recovery models provided clues. Like an open voiced chord, breaking up and matching risk factors to recovery concepts over the risk continuum created a new perspective. Relevance sorts the necessary risk factors at each level of risk.

The following order is sufficient for Mild to Severe Substance Use Disorders.

1. Risk / Benefit
2. Good / Bad
3. New / Familiar
4. Social Proof
5. Control
6. Commitment

These building blocks are useful in this order. Using Frank & Frank's shared components of psychotherapies as a frame, a model can be constructed to combat demoralization (1991, pp. 39-51).

The following overview of these risk factors are part of the Prehab is the New

Rehab presentation and necessary to self assess in the MAPP model.

CHAPTER 6

HOW PERCEPTION WORKS

CC0 pixabay.com

Learning is not something done to students, but rather something students themselves do. It is the direct result of how students interpret and respond to their experiences – conscious and unconscious, past and present (*Ambrose et al., 2010, p. 3*).

Putting risk factors in a progressive model is like having your own personal GPS. The Risk / Benefit factor is the first in this model because it sets the stage for why we do the things we do.

#1 RISK / BENEFIT

#1 RISK / BENEFIT

Because risk factors can increase or decrease fear...

 RISK    BENEFIT

If enough risk factors reduce risk and increase benefit I am doing it.

Humans have a highly evolved capacity to perceive risks related to benefits. It's why we survive and thrive. It's also a perception-driven process.

If I perceive the next action as low risk and high benefit, I'm doing it. If it feels right or I perceive the outcomes as beneficial, I tend to repeat the behavior.

This is a fast response – for reasons related to survival. Why we are so fast but not always accurate is explained by other risk factors.

The next risk factors are also like superpowers. They also tap the mother of all motivators—fear. They instantly increase or decrease risk or benefit based on perceived fear.

The most sublime or absurd behavior happens at the blink of an eye at this level.

The following risk factors determine precisely where our assets turn into liabilities by substituting judgment with perception.

#2 GOOD / BAD

#2 GOOD / BAD

If (anything)
perceived as GOOD

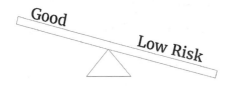

Benefits increase, risk
perception decreases.

The converse is also true: both GOOD and BAD can create fear: fear of loss or missing out.

Good / Bad is like a seesaw. When humans perceive Good, benefits increase and risk decreases. The opposite is also true. Perceiving Bad decreases benefits and increases risk.

This simple risk factor insures our ability to make endless choices extremely fast without exhaustion. There are many seesaws.

Sales, marketing, and political professionals know this.

I will make your life better = good. Vote for me = low risk. If you drive, wear, drink, invest in, smoke, visit, or buy this, it will make you sexy, desirable, powerful, successful, etc. = good and, therefore, high benefit and low risk.

Why didn't I go the beach in 1975? I saw the movie *JAWS*. Eaten alive = bad. Beach = high risk. A no-brainer and also irrational. Yet, part of my brain takes great satisfaction that I remain uneaten.

Having fun is good! Missing out is bad! Our risk levels adjust accordingly. Telling me something is bad merely brings it to my attention, especially if it is new.

#3 NEW/FAMILIAR

Evolution's answer to Google.

#3 NEW / FAMILIAR

What's important?   Is it NEW?

The Unfamiliar commands our attention

Everything else Habituation: an off switch and survival mechanism

Habituation operates in the background which is both, valuable and explains why:
      We cling to the familiar

In the information age we are bombarded with unending and innumerable bits of information from multiple devices.

How to tell what is important?

Creation and evolution graced us with a very fast, accurate, and lifesaving method that never fails.

If it's new, it gets my attention. It's the way we are—a good thing. Check out the drivers next time you're in traffic. No one is paying attention all the time. Anything new in the traffic pattern is noticed faster than the speed of thought.

If I sense movement on my person that did not originate from me, believe me, I investigate at full military throttle until that threat is neutralized. New keeps us safe.

New sells. New demands attention. New generates interest. New arouses desire. Due to this principle some things are investigated that are higher risk and lower benefit than initially perceived.

The flip side of New—Familiar—is just as important.

Imagine a life where it's necessary to relearn everything in your life on a daily basis. Life would be impossible. We simply cannot live without habituation.

Habituation is a superpower. Once something is learned it goes to the background so the foreground can learn some more. This process is repeated for a lifetime.

However, once in the background, it stays there. Resistance to change is profound. We simply lack the ability to focus on the background. We focus outwards. We cling to the familiar, even if we don't want to.

What do we choose to habituate? Any action, perception-driven over a long enough period of time, becomes familiar. Humans can also habituate based on judgment. This also takes time and action.

For dysfunctional habituation there are powerful counseling tools designed to place background material in the foreground where it may be changed. "When Panic Attacks" by David D. Burns MD describes some useful methods for change.

#4 SOCIAL PROOF

Humans don't like ambiguity. We prefer to know the rules and what is going on. A way to combat ambiguity is to observe, and then form conclusions based on immediate perceptions. This results in a kind of conformity called social proof.

This is why people get in a line that forms, then ask, "What are we in line for?" When one person dumps his garbage at the empty lot, others have proof this is a place to dump garbage and act accordingly. Politicians love polls for this reason. Winning! This is how Facebook works. Three hundred forty-one likes? It must be good.

At my first day of college, there were other students there. This was proof that, relative to myself, they were experts. The fact that most of them just arrived and knew nothing did not occur to me.

My tolerance for ambiguity was low; my perception was turned all the way up. Students reduce ambiguity quickly by Social Proof—how the place works, what exactly is permissible as evidenced by what is observed.

Tolerance for ambiguity is not easy or natural. It does guard against irrational social proof and is one reason executives are well paid.

#5 CONTROL

Control less reliable with: #5 CONTROL
Low risk hazards that are encountered frequently.
- Let's camp here!
- Odds are only 1/1000 a tree falls on us tonight
- 1/1000 = Certain death in a few years
- Never sleep next to dead trees = **Constructive Paranoia**

What Kills
People in the
Jungle?

(Diamond, 2013)

What is dangerous for you is lower risk for me, due to control. When you are tired and driving? High-risk. When I am tired and driving? Low-risk.

Control is magnified by our inability to recognize frequently occurring low-risk hazards. Jared Diamond illustrates this principle with trees and older people and shares a dynamic solution to a tricky perception problem (Diamond, 2013).

What kills people in the jungle? Trees. The odds are low—one in a thousand—that a tree will fall on me tonight. Low odds means this is a low risk hazard.

The frequency of occurrence is what makes low risk hazards deadly. People in the jungle know this. The tourists remain blissfully ignorant. One in a thousand odds are not good if 365 days and nights each year are spent in the jungle. Jungle inhabitants discovered a strategy to increase the odds in their favor that is easily applied to many of our risks.

What kills old people? They fall down. Where do they fall down? At home. Where at home? In the bathroom. These are relevant facts to older people as Diamond (2013) points out. Falling at age 75 is different than at age 35. The ability to adjust to increasing hazards or frequency makes a difference. Texting and driving is a similar illustration.

Informing the public that texting and driving is dangerous is good…for others. For me (Control) texting is an added convenience, increases productivity and is encouraged by risk factors like New, Good, Low Risk, High Benefit and Social Proof.

For those who text without consequence, (low-risk hazard) every time they are behind the wheel (frequently occurring), risk increases. Perception cannot change this scenario.

Judgment can. Whether trees, showers, texting, or similar risks there is a foolproof solution. It is called constructive paranoia (Diamond, 2013).

Constructive paranoia nullifies the downside of perception. It requires no energy, cost, loss, or thought. A decision to NEVER sleep next to dead trees, shower casually when old, or text while driving defeats frequently occurring low-risk hazards.

I learned constructive paranoia when shooting clay pigeons with a shotgun on a skeet range. It's impossible to shoot someone by accident if the chamber is always open and empty unless firing at a target. That's the rule. I had no idea how applicable the concept was to the rest of my life—it would have made a difference.

I drive every day. So do many others. I know it's a matter of when, not if, the next accident happens. In order to survive I drive constructively paranoid; seat belt on, no using, no texting and prepared for evasive action.

Constructive paranoia never limits. It just makes getting killed by the familiar less likely. I'm committed to this, which is the next risk factor.

#6 COMMITMENT

Humans have the ability to commit. Commitment is a necessary ingredient for marriage, Philadelphia Eagle fans, rock climbers, or a good golf swing. Our most noble achievements under the most adverse circumstances are powered by commitment.

To say commitment combined with fear

and other risk factors is a runaway train is an understatement.

The Brafman brothers in SWAY: The Irresistible Pull of Irrational Behavior (2008) illustrate how commitment explains SEC football dominance, a failed US Presidency, and the worst accident in aviation history.

I once saw perception-driven commitment at a horse stable. This one horse came with instructions: Never Tie This Horse to Anything. Sure enough, someone didn't get the memo. The instant and explosive large-animal fury resulted in a commitment-driven runaway. As the horse ran, fence remnants at the other end of the rope hit the horse, who then ran faster, resulting in more hitting. Fortunately, there was an unafraid girl this horse apparently trusted, and he stopped when she waved him down, which stopped the hitting.

This is similar to rehab. Increased pain and suffering from substance cessation combined with a righteous commitment to seek relief can be a tedious and sometimes deadly process.

Commitment is also life changing when

combined with an open mind, acceptance and risk factors in a judgment- based process.

This ends the risk factor introduction. These powerful concepts can create or destroy based on one condition; are they perception-driven or judgment-based?

A model is necessary to convert the complex and interesting to the simple and effective.

> Given people's time constraints, effective communication should focus on the issues that recipients most need to understand. If a communication omits critical information, then it fails the most obvious responsibility of communications. It may leave recipients worse off if it creates an illusion of competence, so that recipients erroneously believe themselves to be adequately informed. If it presents irrelevant information then it wastes recipients' time and diverts their attention from more important tasks (Morgan et. al, 2002, p. 4).

The following risk-factor assessment model attempts to integrate these concepts. Self assessment in these stages reveals direction and magnitude of risk over time for your benefit.

It's called Motivational Assessment Prevention Program or MAPP.

CHAPTER 7

THE MAPP MODEL

Learning involves *change* in knowledge, beliefs, behaviors, or attitudes. This change unfolds over time; it is not fleeting but rather has a lasting impact on how students think and act (Ambrose et al., 2010, p. 3).

APP is a stage model. Each row has brief physical, mental, perception and outcome descriptions for each stage. In addition, behavior, overview and going forward notes are included. These are general descriptions that can be complemented by personal experience. Examining each row or stage is preparation for the MAPP assessment. MAPP starts with Stage 0, the first risk level.

STAGE 0

Stage	Physical	Mental	Perception	Outcome
0	No tolerance issues	No obsession issues	Constructive Paranoia Stable Risk / Benefit	No progression No smoking / No drunks Mature judgment
1	No tolerance issues	No obsession issues	New / Good Social Proof	Acute Deaths & Accidents Or to Stage 0 or 2
2	Tolerance adjustment	Impulse	Value Attribution Group Polarization Euphoric Recall Escalation / Commitment	Acute Deaths & Accidents Or to Stage 0 or 3
3	Tolerance peaks	Preoccupation	Familiar / Good Confirmatory Bias Optimistic	Addiction Progression Or to Stage 0 or 4
4	Withdrawal	Obsession	Desperate for Change Cling to Familiar Pain and Suffering Loss Acceptance	Dependence Recovery (abstinence) Or Jails, Institutions, Death

Physical / Mental: Stage 0 has no physical or mental issues.

Perception: Constructive paranoia is activated. Risk / benefit calculations are stable. People here are determined to enjoy life on life's terms; prepared for necessary risks and challenges, and develop tolerance for ambiguity.

Behavior: Nobody smokes anything. Never text and drive. Never sleep next to dead trees. If they drink they don't get drunk or put themselves in jeopardy with those whose judgment is still maturing.

Outcomes: Autonomous, responsible, contributes.

Overview: There is no progression of any kind. Stage 0 has risk because life involves risk. Stage 0 people move into Stage 1 and investigate based on Stage 1 perceptions. They will retain or reject Stage 1 results based on benefit. They return to Stage 0 and prepare to be even more awesome. Seventy-five percent of the population is at Stage 0 or Stage 1.

Going Forward: If judgment based these people continue to maximize benefit and minimize risk from their own experience as well as the experience of others.

If perception-driven, stage one is the beginning of a high risk, low benefit habituation process camouflaged by some good times.

STAGE 1

Stage	Physical	Mental	Perception	Outcome
0	No tolerance issues	No obsession issues	Constructive Paranoia Stable Risk / Benefit	No progression No smoking / No drunks Mature judgment
1	No tolerance issues	No obsession issues	New / Good Social Proof	Acute Deaths & Accidents Or to Stage 0 or 2
2	Tolerance adjustment	Impulse	Value Attribution Group Polarization Euphoric Recall Escalation / Commitment	Acute Deaths & Accidents Or to Stage 0 or 3
3	Tolerance peaks	Preoccupation	Familiar / Good Confirmatory Bias Optimistic	Addiction Progression Or to Stage 0 or 4
4	Withdrawal	Obsession	Desperate for Change Cling to Familiar Pain and Suffering Loss Acceptance	Dependence Recovery (abstinence) Or Jails, Institutions, Death

Physical / Mental: Still no physical or mental issues.

Perception: New, good and social proof are a common and powerful combination. New demands attention, good lowers risk, and social proof removes doubt. We're students; they are having fun. Fun is good; it's bad to miss out. Risk is lowered as perceived benefits increase. The stage is set for high-risk action with a low-risk attitude.

Behavior: Perception-driven exploration

and experimentation with people, places, and things.

Outcomes: Some good times and friendships; some random tragedies related to car accidents, sexual misconduct and alcohol poisoning. A majority of accidents and death occur in Stages 1 and 2.

Overview: Stage 1 is the entrance ramp on the risk continuum and most cruel. Life is taking risks. Everyone experiences Stage 1 risk. Our youngest and most perceptive are most at risk due to a perception-driven process which appears reliable until too late.

Going Forward: Reject low-benefit experiences and retain the high benefit back to Stage 0 or increase velocity in a perception-driven process and advance to Stage 2.

STAGE 2

Stage	Physical	Mental	Perception	Outcome
0	No tolerance issues	No obsession issues	Constructive Paranoia Stable Risk / Benefit	No progression No smoking / No drunks Mature judgment
1	No tolerance issues	No obsession issues	New / Good Social Proof	Acute Deaths & Accidents Or to Stage 0 or 2
2	Tolerance adjustment	Impulse	Value Attribution Group Polarization Euphoric Recall Escalation / Commitment	Acute Deaths & Accidents Or to Stage 0 or 3
3	Tolerance peaks	Preoccupation	Familiar / Good Confirmatory Bias Optimistic	Addiction Progression Or to Stage 0 or 4
4	Withdrawal	Obsession	Desperate for Change Cling to Familiar Pain and Suffering Loss Acceptance	Dependence Recovery (abstinence) Or Jails, Institutions, Death

Physical / Mental: Physical tolerance starts. Human biology expects and adjusts to repeated behavior. More behavior is required to achieve the same results. Impulse is the mental condition. Little to zero thought is required to try something new for any reason at any time.

Perception: Commitment becomes the host to several powerful biases. Loyalty increases because fun, sex, respect, and other values are falsely attributed to the group (value attribution). I earn and maintain my place in the group by doing whatever the group does plus a little bit more. The next members do the same (group polarization). Unplanned extremes become the norm. Everybody remembers the good times, no one remembers the bad times also known as euphoric recall.

Behavior: Pregame, designated drivers, using games, smaller groups, other drugs.

Outcomes: More accidents and deaths combined with longer term consequences like flunking out, Student Conduct citations, and arrests. Progression is under way and will continue in spite of intervention if choices remain perception-driven.

Overview: Stage 2 is a dual threat. Both, acute and chronic symptoms occur here. New is still interesting but experience is hardening into the perceived safety of the familiar; habituation is now primary. Threats to using behavior are threats to benefits, and are resisted vigorously. Strategies to manage outcomes, rather than personal change, start at Stage 2. This is the foundation of a victim stance that results in helplessness.

Going Forward: Begin the process of unwinding low benefits that were once high benefit. Stabilize at stage 0 and re-commit to a judgment-based process (explained further in the next section). Attempting to stay at Stage 2 will result in Stage 3.

STAGE 3

Stage	Physical	Mental	Perception	Outcome
0	No tolerance issues	No obsession issues	Constructive Paranoia Stable Risk / Benefit	No progression No smoking / No drunks Mature judgment
1	No tolerance issues	No obsession issues	New / Good Social Proof	Acute Deaths & Accidents Or to Stage 0 or 2
2	Tolerance adjustment	Impulse	Value Attribution Group Polarization Euphoric Recall Escalation / Commitment	Acute Deaths & Accidents Or to Stage 0 or 3
3	Tolerance peaks	Preoccupation	Familiar / Good Confirmatory Bias Optimistic	Addiction Progression Or to Stage 0 or 4
4	Withdrawal	Obsession	Desperate for Change Cling to Familiar Pain and Suffering Loss Acceptance	Dependence Recovery (abstinence) Or Jails, Institutions, Death

Physical / Mental: Physical tolerance can't get any higher. Massive quantities are normal, extremes are preferred. Preoccupation sets in. Planning to use, using, and recovering from using become routine and priority #1. Regardless of importance, everything else is a distant second. This outcome is obvious to all except the user.

Perception: Risk factors at Stage 3 include familiar, confirmatory bias, and optimism. At this stage anything new is at the expense of the familiar and therefore avoided. No matter the desire of the individual—new semester, new school, new relationships, new habits, or new plans—the familiar wins out. Examples of confirmatory biases include statements like: Alcohol has health benefits. Alcohol is much more dangerous than weed. Weed saves lives. There are more old drunks than there are old doctors.

In spite of the increased quantity and magnitude of consequences, users at Stage 3 can be absurdly optimistic. Like the gambler's fallacy, they believe they are due, if they just stay the course. When change is needed most, it is feared most, an insidious paradox.

Behavior: Wake and bake, naming your bong, Beer pong with Tequila. Bars are preferred meeting places and landmarks. Other drugs become compensatory. Chemical assistance becomes necessary for basic activities and goals: sleep, eat, get up, study, lose weight, clean the house, focus, increase strength, rest, enjoy, and the list goes on.

Outcomes: Acute risks are reduced—Stage 3 people know better, they are beyond rookie mistakes. Risk for addiction and related consequences increase by the minute in Stage 3.

Overview: Stage 3 looks like addiction but it's not. It is close. Enough time at Stage 3 will result in Stage 4 addiction. Stopping and starting can change tolerance and lead to overdose in Stage 3 or 4.

Going Forward: Disease is setting in. Change can and does happen. Stage 0 happens when Stage 3 people accurately self-assess, face fear, and commit to action to the best of their abilities through a judgment-based process. Otherwise the natural progression for Stage 3 is Stage 4.

STAGE 4

Stage	Physical	Mental	Perception	Outcome
0	No tolerance issues	No obsession issues	Constructive Paranoia Stable Risk / Benefit	No progression No smoking / No drunks Mature judgment
1	No tolerance issues	No obsession issues	New / Good Social Proof	Acute Deaths & Accidents Or to Stage 0 or 2
2	Tolerance adjustment	Impulse	Value Attribution Group Polarization Euphoric Recall Escalation / Commitment	Acute Deaths & Accidents Or to Stage 0 or 3
3	Tolerance peaks	Preoccupation	Familiar / Good Confirmatory Bias Optimistic	Addiction Progression Or to Stage 0 or 4
4	Withdrawal	Obsession	Desperate for Change Cling to Familiar Pain and Suffering Loss Acceptance	Dependence Recovery (abstinence) Or Jails, Institutions, Death

Physical / Mental: Withdrawal / Obsession or Addiction

Perception: Desperate for change, will not let go of the familiar. Pain and suffering; loss acceptance. No fear of death, terrified of living.

Behavior: Constant attempts at control; can always stop, can never stay stopped. Changes lanes on the addiction highway—instead of changing.

Outcomes: Death, institutions, or change.

Overview: An unchecked perception-driven process over time destroys our best and affects everyone else. The level of commitment and determination necessary to reach this end of the continuum is rare. Only 5% of the population get this far. At some point all addicts attempt to control or stop using. Withdrawal sets in. All drugs have varying degrees of withdrawal. Pain and suffering increase. Relief is sought through use, further increasing pain and suffering, resulting in cessation again, which further increases pain and suffering. Without change this cycle ends in overdose, imprisonment, or death.

Going Forward: Like all other stages, adopt a judgment-based process at Stage 0 – after or while undergoing the appropriate combination of detox and treatment. Not many make it to this level. Not everyone gets out. I believe everyone gets a moment of clarity. Be prepared. Chapter 11 is a modified version of MAPP to assist stage 4 people back to stage 0. Recovered people learn they can be of service when no one else can. Their worst stuff, in a short period of time, is transformed into their best stuff. Like the addiction process itself, regaining health takes time and persistence.

CHAPTER 8

FIND YOUR RISK LEVEL AND UNDERSTAND THEIRS

CC0 stocksnap.com

Stages in a model, like a compass, help us navigate. Stages over time tell us where we were, where we are, where we are going. This informs us how far and how fast we have traveled.

Information is leverage. When combined with useful action over time judgment develops. Autonomy is the result.

Gather some information. Use the MAPP assessment below.

THE MAPP ASSESSMENT

Fill in each blank below with a MAPP stage number.

    1. What stage were you at?   _____

    2. What stage are you at?   _____

    3. What stage will you be at?   _____

The answers in the above assessment form a special variable known as the Temporal Assessment Variable (TAV). The TAV indicates direction and magnitude of risk over time. Combining the first response with the second and third responses forms the TAV. For example: I was at stage 0, I am at stage 1, I will be at stage 0 yields a score of 010.

A TAV of 230 means I was at stage 2, I am at stage 3, I will be at stage 0. TAV scores can be categorized in terms of perception and judgment.

TAV SCORES

The 3-digit TAV identifies your personal perception-driven trajectory and the degree to which perception is either used as judgment or serves judgment. Scores vary.

There are three trends that do not change. The following categories represent the general rules that repeatedly occur in a random sample – even among college freshmen.

1. Maintenance Category 75% of scores will end in 1 or 0. For instance a 000, 111, or 101.
2. Intervention Category 20% of scores will end in 1 or 0 after a higher middle

score. Like a 010, 121, 321, 440, and so on.

3. Prevention Category   5% of scores will end in 2 or above, as in 122, 222, 123, 332, 323, or 444.

The next three sections briefly describe each of these categories.

The Maintenance Category (75%)

This group represents both the most developed students and the students most at risk. Most people in this category learned to use habituation for personal gain and continue to investigate, reject, or retain those people, places, and things that interest them and compliment their purpose. Outcomes are positive, high degrees of success are possible and likely.

Yet most accidents and deaths will occur in this group. The reasons are: first, the large size of the group and secondly, not everyone is developed. How to tell the highly developed from the high risk when everyone behaves low risk at the moment?

One way to tell is if perception is used as judgment. Caution is good. Reflecting the low risk behavior around you is good. Both attitudes are low risk but perception-driven and insufficient to deal with change. Over time, perception cannot replace judgment without consequence.

Risk / benefit choices are stable when it's all good. Anybody can fly in fair weather. I want a pilot with judgment when the weather, mechanical failure, or something else becomes a factor.

There will always be risk factors like new, good and social proof which modify perception. As perception is modified so is caution. The most tragic fatalities happen here. They never see it coming, everyone is sorry, nothing changes.

Increasing development in this population prevents most unnecessary tragedy and wreckage. The next chapter specifically illustrates risk perception factors in service of judgment.

The Intervention Category (20%)

Most people in this category look low risk. They believe they are low risk. In some ways they are low risk.

They survived the rookie mistakes, learned from those who didn't make it or rely on caution alone. Some in this category will proudly counsel others how to avoid risk which lays the foundation for chronic issues.

Low risk due to experience is a small consolation because dysfunctional habituation develops by the moment.

Over time unavoidable consequences happen. Most people in this category will adjust. The cost of developing in this manner for some is costly, extreme and tragic.

Some will continue to rely on perception. Their defenses harden and relief becomes the primary objective.

Life is not easy for anyone. Discouragement happens. Discouragement in this category is deadly because the solution is just a drink, toke, hit, purge, orgasm or purchase away.

Developing the affective response system

through accurate self assessment can be enough for the intuitive members in this group.

Change at this level ends progression before addiction. The next chapter provides more leverage and clarity.

The Prevention Category (5%)

This is the smallest population. They are usually the brightest and most creative. Some are still enjoying the ride. Many are experiencing various levels of demoralization. Change at the severe end of the spectrum too often never happens. Timing matters.

Most responses in this category going forward are between stage 2 and stage 4. That's why this category is called prevention. Accurate self assessment in this category is an opportunity to choose rather than blindly progress.

Which ones make it? No one can tell. The lower risk stage 2s and 3s may find change more challenging than stage 4 people. Change is rare for the high functioning person who feels good, looks good and enjoys real or imagined benefits.

Fear based perception always attributes some self serving rationale to success or failure. This process provides a false, fragile but secure effect. This kind of attribution error destroys our best. Developing judgment is the more beneficial path.

For those that have lost everything change is sometimes easier to consider. This does not mean all consequences result in change. Consequences sometimes result in the construction and hardening of defenses. Reliance on relief becomes primary—the heart of the perception-driven model.

In either case taking responsibility for your own affective response system cannot fail. It will take courage. The same risk factors that result in Moderate and Severe Use Disorders can also result in a judgment-based process.

For anyone interested in learning more about stage 4 and recovery see chapter 11.

In summary, the perception-driven suffer twice. The majority get randomly picked off, the minority progress into addiction. The loss of life and productivity are staggering; everyone suffers.

What can be done? What's the path from perception-driven to judgment-based? That's the purpose of the next few pages.

Perception risk factors can destroy or develop. The key to development is not reducing risk but maximizing benefit.

CHAPTER 9

LOW BENEFIT PERCEPTION PROBLEM

If you focus on results you will never change, (first half of quote) *-Jack Dixon*

LOW BENEFIT RISK FACTORS

Perception-Driven Risk / Benefit Cycle

Duncan Park Press LLC

	High Benefit	Low Benefit
Low Risk	Stage 0. Improve purpose, take action in stage 1 Constructive Paranoia	Stage 2. Value Attribution, Group Polarization, Commitment Stage 3. Familiar, Good Confirmatory Bias Decreased acute, Increased chronic consequences
High Risk	Stage 1. New, Good, Social Proof Increased acute and chronic consequences	Stage 4. Cling to familiar, Pain and Suffering, Loss Acceptance Addiction

Results cannot be managed into change; they can inform the benefit quality of risk factors as seen in the above model.

The MAPP stages in a risk/ benefit matrix portrays what the undeveloped affective response system looks like in modern times.

A perception-driven cycle is progressive. Everyone starts in stage 0. Without intervention, perception based action results in stage 4 over time. This is the problem.

Analyzing the MAPP stages in terms of risk and benefit breaks down the problem. The rows reveal risk by stage; the columns show benefit by stage.

MAPP STAGES BY RISK

Stages 0, 2 and 3 populate the low risk row. Stages 1 and 4 are high risk. The prevention paradox validates this pattern.

Besides unavoidable risk, stage 0 is as low risk as one can get. There will be times to increase risk – that is stage 1.

For acute consequences Stages 2 and 3 reduce risk. These users are experienced, in some ways less risky. It's almost like judgment. It is not. The valid perception of low acute risk while increasing chronic risk is deadly.

Stage 4 is high risk for everything: Severe Substance Use Disorders, losses, incarceration, misery and death.

There is always increasing and decreasing risk in life. Everyone prepares for this eventuality by perception in this model because it works – in the short term. The problem is loss of choice regarding progression.

Behavior based on accumulating risk factors guarantee habituation over time. There is no managing risk and perception in this model; risk and perception manage us. Autonomy is not possible. Dependence is inevitable.

MAPP STAGES BY BENEFIT

Stages by benefits are seen by columns. Stages 1 and 0 are high benefit. Stages 2, 3 and 4 are low benefit. This is a reasonable interpretation over time.

Time takes into account the illusion of high benefit. This illusion happens mostly in stages 1 and 2. This is when instant gratification combines with risk factors in the short term inflating benefit for a while.

These benefits are never maintained. At stages 3 and 4 habituation sets in after perceived benefits are long gone.

Stages 2, 3 and 4 generate the outcomes of using perception as judgment: skewed risk, low benefit and progression.

This is the hallmark of progressive disorders; clinging to the familiar, waiting for benefits that will never return in a high-risk setting. What is settled for in order to maintain the familiar is beyond pitiful and outrageous.

Only one element in this model is possible to manage; risk factors themselves. Although risk factors cannot

> Benefits are no more manageable than risk in this model.

be directly amplified or diminished, how we use them is 100% up to us.

Managing risk factors creates power, responsibility and judgment. A small change can change everything as seen in the next model.

Chapter 10

PERCEPTION IS HIGH BENEFIT LEVERAGE

… if you focus on change you will get results. (second half of quote) *-Jack Dixon*

Judgment-Based Risk / Benefit Cycle		
	High Benefit	Low Benefit
Low Risk	Stage 0. Improve purpose, take action in stage 1 Constructive Paranoia Commitment, Familiar, Group Polarization, Confirmatory Bias Principles, Autonomy	Stage 2. Stage 3. Reduced and eliminated by Stage 1
High Risk	Stage 1. New, Good, Social Proof, Pain and Suffering, Loss Acceptance Retain High Benefit return to 0. Reject Low Benefit return to 0.	Stage 4. Eliminated to the degree Stage 2 and 3 are reduced.

Duncan Park Press LLC

The solution is more high-benefit risk factors. Focus on this change gets results.

Migrating low-benefit risk factors to the high-benefit column places perception in service of judgment, as evidenced by a high-benefit lifestyle at the expense of low-benefit outcomes, like Substance Use Disorders.

There is no judgment without perception. Therefore, judgment is best served by perception early and often.

This order maximizes the benefit of perception when it is needed most. The most destructive Stage 2, 3 and 4 risk factors are transformed in Stage 0 and Stage 1.

Making decisions, even bad ones, is a good thing in a judgment – based model. It's how we learn. It's how we increase our tolerance for tension and ambiguity. The courage to be imperfect drives development. The probability for desirable outcomes increases.

STAGE 0 HIGH BENEFIT

Stage 0 becomes a solid foundation for autonomy. It's where commitment is used for process rather then outcomes. Principle based action is firm and familiar. Autonomous people are not easily distracted or taken advantage of.

In stage 0 constructive paranoia is habituated. Adult boundaries form. A high benefit bias has little downside – it is a bias against low benefit.

We pick and serve our groups based on our gifts using both perception and judgment. A lot of time and energy is saved for worthy purposes. Good times become part of living rather than compensation for misery.

Security is significantly increased at little – if any cost. The probability of frequently occurring low risk hazards is reduced.

Stage 0 is home, safe, where we rest, enjoy life and prepare for more risk.

STAGE 1 HIGH BENEFIT

Stage 1 trades risk for benefit ensuring continued development. The time comes to investigate what is new and perceived as good as an individual or group.

This is the reality check for perceived high benefit bias. Prepare, investigate risk, analyze the benefit then take action. This is not an impulsive process, it is thoughtful. Logic, value and other earthlings must be taken into account.

If the benefit is worth the risk, then make it familiar at Stage 0.

If low benefit or too risky to habituate, then reject, learn, and prepare for something better.

Exercising retention or rejection based on
benefit at Stage 1 guarantees judgment-based
development.   Our   natural   perception
superpowers now aid rather than destroy.

Action along these lines are not always
pleasant or pleasurable. There are losses.
There is pain and suffering. Return to Stage
0, process loss, continue the journey.

It's only when we attempt to avoid pain
and suffering do they become permanent.
Accepted as part of life – these things become
necessary and temporary. After all, but for
the bad times there would be no good times.

None of us are born knowing all our gifts
and exact purpose. Too often both are wasted
in a perception-driven process. Persistent
judgment-based action over time results in
development of gifts and clarity of purpose.

It is predictable, regardless of risk, that a
perception-driven process over time is low
benefit and results in use disorders.

Likewise, regardless of risk, a judgment-
based process is high benefit and precludes
the primary criteria for use disorders: low
benefit patterns over time. Different people

develop at different times as they face life challenges. Whatever your experience, continue to do good. Stay high benefit for your well being and those you contact.

CHAPTER 11

RECOVERY MAPP

If you find yourself in a hole…

The following few words review change and the MAPP and judgment models adjusted for recovery. This section can be an aid, it is not a substitute for treatment or counseling. Cooperation with professionals and recovered people create opportunities for judgment-based actions. Judgment-based actions lead to change.

The level of pain in chronic addiction can be psychic in nature. Psychic pain has no boundaries. Self harm or suicide will appear attractive. Do not be fooled.

Psychic pain is neither real nor permanent, it is fear. Attempts to think out of this corner is like putting out a fire with gasoline.

The way out is persistent, small, right actions; the opposite of fear based perception – driven thinking. See the "fear sheet" in Appendix I to recognize and reduce thinking errors.

The time to feel, think and act has passed. Thought is entertainment at this stage. Something to be watched for a laugh and perhaps learn from.

The time to act based on principles has

come. Responsible action results in different feelings. Fear dissolves. Over a persistent trial – thinking is re-habituated.

If desperate, call 911 or The National Suicide Hotline: 800-273-8255. The nearest 12 step meeting can be found at www.aa.org. The recovered people there can show you exactly how to avoid the traps of early recovery.

Note: If you like the meetings – great. The meetings are not the program. The meetings are the fellowship. The Alcoholics Anonymous book, also known as the big book, is the program. Follow the directions in the big book and and you get your life back.

Al-Anon, www.al-anon.org , is the 12 step group for those who love someone with an addiction disorder. They have similar directions.

Confusing religion and spirituality is an understandable, perception-driven, fear based strategy to avoid change. Keep taking responsible action. Face Everything And Recover.

The following are suggestions based on

the MAPP model as guides to Stage 0 and a judgment-based perspective.

STAGE 4

Prehab is the New **Rehab**   Recovery MAPP

Stage	Physical	Mental	Perception	Outcome
4	Detox / Abstain	Limit thinking to current responsible contributions.	Limit Perception to personal responsibilities.	Mourn losses Prepare for action
1	Maintain Abstinence	Acceptance / Logic and Values Check	New / Good Social Proof High risk / High Benefit.	Take baby steps (action) Trust Acceptance
0	Maintain Abstinence	Rely on principles / judgment	Constructive Paranoia Stable Risk / Benefit Commitment	Autonomy No relapse Mature judgment Execute purpose

Physical / Mental: Detox and take a break from thinking. It just turns into mind racing unless thinking is used to either help someone else or follow responsible directions. It gets better.

Perception: As little as possible. Staying in the moment is going to be a full-time job for a little while. Use your perception for right now, not yesterday, not tomorrow, right now.

Use materials like the "fear sheet" in Appendix I on a daily, hourly or minute by minute basis as needed.

Behavior: Do the next right thing or do

nothing at all.

Outcomes: Change brings losses. Unmourned losses accumulate. Mourned losses always lead to good. Mourn losses by talking…not acting. Talk to others who can listen without advising.

Overview: Do not do this alone. Get help from friends, family, professionals, or a 12-step group. This is the end of perception-driven and the beginning of judgment-based. It's not going to feel good all the time. Feeling good is no longer your purpose. Feelings come and go. Your job is to show up and do the next right thing.

Going Forward: The time spent preparing for Stage 1 depends on how much damage was done in stage 4.

If you are physically free of mood-altering substances and you can follow simple directions—it is probably time for Stage 1.

STAGE 1

Prehab is the New **Rehab**   Recovery MAPP

Stage	Physical	Mental	Perception	Outcome
4	Detox / Abstain	Limit thinking to current responsible contributions.	Limit Perception to personal responsibilities.	Mourn losses Prepare for action
1	Maintain Abstinence	Acceptance / Logic and Values Check	New / Good Social Proof High risk / High Benefit.	Take baby steps (action) Trust Acceptance
0	Maintain Abstinence	Rely on principles / judgment	Constructive Paranoia Stable Risk / Benefit Commitment	Autonomy No relapse Mature judgment Execute purpose

Physical / Mental: Maintain abstinence. Stay on your side of the street. Accept people, places and things. If you can't name a principle or value based on your next action, it's not beneficial, no matter what the voices say. The voices in this context represent our fearful childlike parts. It is not necessary to fight the voices. Be gentle. Be loving. Be very firm. The surprising power of the "acceptance paradox" (Burns, 2006, p. 214) and other useful techniques are explained and demonstrated in *When Panic Attacks.*

Perception: Time for your superpowers to

work for you. Investigate the new (recovery meetings), good (recovery program) and social proof (recovered people). Use your perception to relate and contribute. Not everything will go your way. There will be suffering; it's part of life. The time for misery is over.

Behavior: Doing the next right thing at this stage is going to require courage and more courage. Taking responsible action is not always easy. At times —for a few seconds—it may take maximum effort. Once action is started it gets easier by the second. This kind of courage results in outcomes not yet imagined.

Outcomes: This is the new and exciting part of recovery. You will have high points and low points. If persistent, this pattern moderates into an upward trajectory. You will begin to experience the ability to give yourself enough time to be honest enough to retain high-benefit actions and reject low-benefit actions. Mistakes, pain, emotions are all useful now—they let you know what is real.

Overview: Change has started—not done yet.

Keep going.

Going Forward: Prolonged action in Stage 1 will let you know what to reject and what to keep. Managing the voices removes the primary barrier to recovery – self centered fear.

Consistent action results in Stage 0.

STAGE 0

Prehab is the New **Rehab**   Recovery MAPP

Stage	Physical	Mental	Perception	Outcome
4	Detox / Abstain	Limit thinking to current responsible contributions.	Limit Perception to personal responsibilities.	Mourn losses Prepare for action
1	Maintain Abstinence	Acceptance / Logic and Values Check	New / Good Social Proof High risk / High Benefit.	Take baby steps (action) Trust Acceptance
0	Maintain Abstinence	Rely on principles / judgment	Constructive Paranoia Stable Risk / Benefit Commitment	Autonomy No relapse Mature judgment Execute purpose

Physical / Mental: Maintain abstinence. Reliance on something other than perception has formed.

Perception: The very risk factors that destroy addicts now guarantee recovery. Stage 0 is a high-benefit, low-risk stage. Live well.

Behavior: Your experience, strengths, and abilities are known, trusted, and useful to others. Continue to show up and give of yourself in a judgment-based manner.

Outcomes: Successful living in good times or bad. The ability to tolerate an occasional perception-driven thought rather than acting on it.

Overview: Fearlessly move between Stages 0 and 1.

Going Forward: Your actions are contagious. The world is a better place due to your existence.

CHAPTER 12

HOW TO END IT

There is little evidence that education interventions in the Alcohol and Other Drug field are effective *(Babor et al. 2010, p. 216; Correia, et al. 2012, pp. 18, 306).*

Despite differences in specific content, all therapeutic myths and rituals have functions in common. They combat demoralization by strengthening the therapeutic relationship, inspiring expectations of help, providing new learning experiences, arousing the patient emotionally, enhancing a sense of mastery or self efficacy and affording opportunities for rehearsal and practice (Frank & Frank, 1991, p. 44).

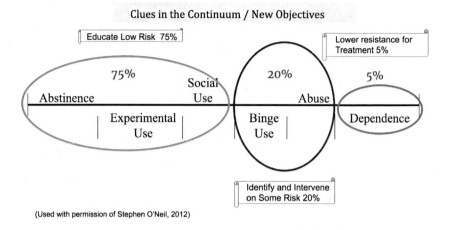

(Used with permission of Stephen O'Neil, 2012)

As suggested in the first citation, something is not working in AOD education. Applying the latest perception research along with the concepts found in the second citation encourages development.

It is not enough to focus on the high risk.

In order for effective education to impact individuals, groups and cultures, continuum based objectives and collaboration must be considered.

The objectives are described next, followed by the best method to realize the objectives – collaboration.

EDUCATE LOW RISK

Whether in high school or college the low-risk majority (75%) are still at risk. The low risk can still be perception-driven.

It is not the high-risk who die from alcohol poisoning or related incidents on a college campus. Tragically, the low risk population at great cost, experience fatal errors year after year. Due to selection bias, there are no "low risk" assessments. Until now.

Educating the low risk about themselves and others, (friends, family, and acquaintances), while encouraging a judgment-based trajectory is perhaps the most powerful, different, and effective objective to reduce progression now, and therefore addiction in the future.

~~~

IDENTIFY AND INTERVENE THE SOME RISK

> It is no longer necessary to wait for accidents, mental illness, sexual assault, dysfunction, or legal and financial issues to indicate there may be a problem.

20% of the population is neither low-risk or high-risk. They represent the "some" risk. The some risk present a different challenge. They are invisible because they look low risk and are treated low risk until evidence suggests otherwise – which is too late.

If consequences are avoided or ignored long enough, progression insures some combination of tragic consequence and addiction. Time is not on their side. Current assessments are not designed for this group.

Risk perception errors are different at this level. Enticing benefits without much risk are very seductive; especially when combined with sex, intimacy, fellowship, camaraderie, friendship, community, and other new experiences. A desire for more of the same leads to commitment, which leads to progression, regardless of consequences.

For the first time a new objective is possible. The objective is to identify and intervene before acute or chronic consequences occur. The discovery of how to do this is the reason for this book.

In random samples, repeated MAPP interventions indicate the predictable 20% some risk can be identified and intervened on. No one else has this objective, let alone supporting evidence of reaching it.

~~~

LOWER RESISTANCE FOR HIGH-RISK

A minority (five percent) of the population will experience Severe Substance Use Disorders. Effective intervention at earlier stages prevent addiction. Intervention at stages 2 – 4 prevents progression and reduces resistance to treatment.

Prehab TAV scores plainly indicate levels of the high risk struggle: a desire to avoid both Stage 4 and Stage 0. Over time, without intervention, stage 4 is the result.

Due to perception, traditional assessments do not have a broad application – even at high levels of risk. The assessment process is sometimes like the reply of the man who was asked how he was doing at the 5th floor after he fell off the 10th floor roof – "so far, so good". The next assessment is likely to be more accurate and too late.

Hopeful ignorance quickly fades in assessments based on perception risk factors.

Every future outcome will indicate movement towards or away from a judgment – based process. Cognitive dissonance and education results in healthy change when a clear path to re habituation is available.

Students at severe substance use levels tend to be experienced. They are desperate for the right information and will take action if resistance is not aroused or their time wasted.

At Kennesaw State University, 5 out of 457 first semester freshman students self-assessed at Stage 4, after a one-hour presentation from a peer educator in a classroom activity. This is a dramatic outcome without the drama.

These students knew something was wrong. They learned through their own interpretation of the presentation facts based on their own experience. That's the benefit of an educational assessment.

Early intervention in an expert model avoids the "expert" and similar traps that encourage dependency (Miller & Rollnick, 2002, pp. 55-63).

Too often the struggle continues until all resources are exhausted and prognosis becomes grim. The only real way to advance the combat against demoralization related to substance use is through continuum-based objectives. Collaboration makes it real for the culture.

*

COLLABORATION

Not everyone has to participate in Prehab for a culture to benefit. This explains why a fraction of participating students impacted a campus wide measurement.

At any give time, most students are low risk. The challenge is not contact with every student, but contacting the right students at the right time. Collaboration makes this possible.

Students will carry the solution – if they have one. A brief analysis of experience with the following groups builds a strong case for collaboration in schools and communities. Collaboration allows everyone to participate and take credit for reduced negative outcomes.

~~~

FRESHMAN ORIENTATION

Efforts to increase retention start with a good foundation. Universities have a first-year programs for this reason.

A one-hour intervention for the Freshman

class puts everyone on the same page when New, Good, and Social Proof are rampant and most influential. Repeating the exercise every spring and fall changes the culture before the first participating freshmen class graduates.

All three objectives are maximized at the Freshman orientation level. Intervening on the low-risk, some-risk and high-risk has immediate and long-term benefits for families, school, community and future students.

~~~

MANDATED EDUCATION

Mandated education has a larger than expected effect for several reasons. First, CYAAR did not have to screen 25,714 students. Student Conduct and Academic Integrity policies in conjunction with faculty, police and staff produced the students we were interested in. When staff realized through student feedback the benefits of the mandated class trust and collaboration increased.

Another benefit of mandated education is measurable. When students are fined and mandated they drop their risk level – for a while. MAPP measures another drop in risk level after the Prehab presentation. This category is called pre intervention.

As seen in Table 3, the pre intervention and pre risk student types represent 50% of this sample. All but 8% responded to the intervention or stayed in the maintenance category.

The high risk and low risk are the other 50% of this sample. There is change for these groups also – not nearly as much as the top two categories.

Table 3

Mandated Intervention by Student Type Variable

Mandated Class	Fall 2014 n=84			
	Intervention	Maintenance	Prevention	Total
Pre Intervention	17%	11%	2%	30%
Pre Risk	13%	1%	6%	20%
High Risk	7%	0%	12%	19%
Low Risk	6%	25%	0%	31%
Total	43%	37%	20%	100%

Once again there is evidence that the middle of the continuum will respond – if you can find them. Mandated education finds them and those hanging around them.

Change in these students impacts their existing groups now and the culture over time. The influential students are still influential—in a more informed way. Good for them, good for the groups, good for the culture.

Lastly, from time to time a fear will surface among some educators that collaboration is somehow redundant. What they mean is repetitive.

The fear is that a freshmen could self assess in freshmen orientation, greek life, health class, in the dorms and a mandated class resulting in boredom.

The Prehab presentation delivered by different people in different formats to the same students in different groups is affective according to student comments and reduced negative consequences. Repetition is good if the information is useful.

~~~

SELECTED GROUPS

Selected groups like Athletes or Greek Life are similar to mandated groups with one important difference. Not everyone in a mandated group knows everyone else.

Chances are in a selected group everyone knows everyone—really well. Everyone knows exactly what stage and experience everyone else has had, is having, and likely to have. It's really a group intervention.

MAPP is a non-judgmental method to explain progression and is generally safe to use in these environments. MAPP is not a substitute for counseling services including assessment for self harm and referral to a higher level of care.

Sometimes groups are both selected and mandated – which can be even more powerful. I have seen fraternities effectively confront Severe Substance Use as a brotherhood during a mandated Prehab presentation.

~~~

CONCLUSION

Will perception be used as judgment or in service of judgment? This is an important question better answered sooner than later.

Education is change if facts are presented that students relate to and use to develop their own affective response systems. The empowerment model is no longer just a theory.

New theories and models lead to new applications, measurements and conclusions. Change is good when autonomy is the result.

A judgment-based process is empowerment.

ABOUT THE AUTHOR

COMBATING DEMORALIZATION

Patrick Noble Moore M.A. LPC

———

Pat is a Licensed Professional Counselor, creator of the Motivational Assessment Prevention Program (MAPP) and Prehab presentation designed to combat demoralization through education and anonymous self assessment.

Pat's research focuses on the risk continuum for Substance Use Disorders from prevention to treatment. His research uncovered causes and effective education methods for all risk levels as evidenced by reduced negative consequences. His research experience is complemented by his clinical experience with Individual Psychology, Cognitive Behavior Therapy and Myers-Briggs Type Indicator. Pat is a contributing member and speaker for conferences and continuing education.

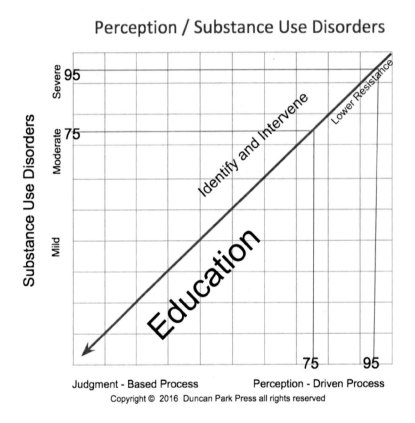

Perception / Substance Use Disorders

Inquiries regarding conferences, seminars or training are welcome. Prehab can be bought in bulk at special discounts for educational purposes through contacting Duncan Park Press.

Patrick N. Moore LPC
Duncan Park Press LLC
4555 Mansell Road, Suite 300
Alpharetta, GA 30022
Phone: 770-521-4212
Fax: 770-521-4200
Email:pm@prehabmapp.com
www.duncanparkpress.com

APPENDIX I FEAR SHEET

DESPAIR, HOPELESSNESS, FEAR

THE BIG, BIG PROBLEM(S)

Author Unknown: Courtesy of John G. and the Big Kahuna

1. Don't live in the problem!

2. Concentrate on the SOLUTION. Don't even think about THE PROBLEM for one second.

3. This too shall pass.

4. ACCEPT what's going on – I don't have to like it!

5. Deal with disasters or problems WHEN they happen. NOT before if I'm not able to do anything about them today.

6. Don't magnify or analyze the problems by thinking about them. Quit THINKING! Quit ANTICIPATING!

7. Remove or lower my expectations. Don't anticipate or predict the future.

8. If I can't do anything about the problems today put them aside till tomorrow. If I can do anything today about one or any of the problems today, DO IT WITHOUT DELAY.

9. Forget what is going on in my head – where are my feet going?

10. Continue with my self-discipline, ENDURE to the end.

11. Whatever happens it's not going to kill me.

12. I only have to carry this load till bedtime tonight.

REFERENCES

Ambrose, Susan A. Bridges, Michael W. DiPietro, Michele, Lovett, Marsha C. Norman, Marie K. (2010). How Learning Works 7 Research-Based Principles for Smart Teaching. San Francisco, CA: John Wiley & Sons, Inc.

Babbie, Earl. (2004). The Practice of Social Research. (10th ed.). Belmont, CA. Wadsworth/Thomson Learning.

Babor, Thomas; Caetano, Raul; Casswell, Sally; Griffith, Edwards; Giesbrecht, Norman; Graham, Kathryn; Grube, Joel; Hill, Linda; Holder, Harold; Homel, Ross; Livingston, Michael; Osterberg, Esa; Rehm, Jurgen; Room, Robin; Rossow, Ingeborg. (2010). Alcohol: No Ordinary Commodity Research and public policy second edition. New York, New York: Oxford University Press Inc.

Babor, Thomas F. Higgins-Biddle, John C.

(2001). Brief Intervention For Hazardous and Harmful Drinking, A Manual for Use in Primary Care. World Health Organization, Department of Mental Health and Substance Dependence. WHO/MSD/MSB/01.6b

Barlow, David H., Durand, Mark V. (2005). Abnormal Psychology: An Integrative Approach. (4th ed.). Belmont, CA: Wadsworth Publishing

Bazerman, Max H., Tenbrunsel, Ann E. (2011). Blind Spots Why We Fail to Do What's Right and What to Do about It. Princeton, N.J: Princeton University Press.

Brafman, Ori and Brafman, Rom. (2008). SWAY The Irresistible Pull of Irrational Behavior. NewYork, New York: Doubleday.

Burns, David D. (2006). When Panic Attacks: The new drug-free anxiety therapy that can change your life. New York: Broadway Books

Chickering, Arthur W., Reisser, Linda (1993). Education and Identity. San Francisco, CA: Jossey-Bass Inc.

Correia, Christopher J., Murphy, James G. and Barnett, Nancy P. (2012). College

Student Alcohol Abuse: A guide to Assessment, Intervention, and Prevention. New Jersey: John Wiley & Sons.

Cummings, Sheila. (2001). An Empowerment Model for Collegiate Substance Abuse Prevention and Education Programs. Rochester, NY: University of Rochester.

Diamond, Jared. (January 28, 2013). That Daily Shower Can Be a Killer. New York Times, Science Section, New York, New York.

Frank, Jerome D., Frank, Julia B. (1991). Persuasion and Healing. A Comparative Study of Psychotherapy. (3rd ed.). Baltimore, Maryland: The Johns Hopkins University Press.

Gardner, Daniel. (2008). The Science of Fear Why We Fear the Things We Shouldn't – and Put Ourselves in Greater Danger. New York, New York: Dutton, Penguin Group (USA) Inc.

Howard, George S, and Nathan, Peter E. (1994). Alcohol Use and Misuse By Young Adults. Notre Dame, Indiana: University of Notre Dame Press,

Kreitman, Norman, M.D. , F.R.C.P.,

F.R.C.Psych. (1986). Alcohol Consumption and the Preventive Paradox. British Journal of Addiction (1986) 81, 353-363.

Kahneman, Daniel. (2011). Thinking Fast and Slow. New York, NY: Farrar, Straus and Giroux.

Livio, Mario (2013). Brilliant Blunders From Darwin to Einstein Colossal Mistakes by Great Scientists That Changed Our Understanding of Life and the Universe. New York, New York: Simon & Schuster

Manaster, Guy J. Corsini, Raymond J. Individual Psychology. Theory and Practice. (1982). US: Adler School of Professional Psychology

McLeod, John. (2003). Doing Counseling Research. (2nd ed.). London England: Sage Publications Ltd

Miller, William R. Rollnick, Stephen. (2002). Motivational Interviewing Preparing People for Change. (2nd ed.). New York, NY: The Guilford Press.

Morgan, Granger M., Fischhoff, Baruch., Bostrom, Ann., & Atman, Cynthia J. (2002). Risk Communications: A Mental Model

Approach. New York, NY: Cambridge University Press

Myers, Isabel Briggs, Myers, Peter B. (1995). Gifts Differing. Mountain View, CA: Davies-Black Publishing

Pinker, Steven. (2002). The Blank Slate. The Modern Denial of Human Nature. New York, NY: Penguin Books

Ropeik, David. (2010). How Risky Is It, Really? Why Our Fears Don't Always Match the Facts. New York, New York: McGraw Hill.

Rose, Geoffrey. (1981). Strategy of prevention: lessons from cardiovascular disease. Brit Med J; 282:1847-51

Sandman, Peter M. (2009). Climate Change Risk Communication: The Problem of Psychological Denial. www.psandman.com

Schinke, Steven P., Gilbert ,Botvin J. , Orlandi, Mario A. (1991). Substance Abuse in Children and Adolescents. Newbury Park, CA: Sage Publications Inc.

Smagorinsky, P., Cook L. S., & Johnson, T. S. (2003). The Twisting Path of Concept Development in Learning to Teach. Albany, NY: CELA.

Spurling, Maria C.; Vinson Daniel C. (2005). Alcohol-Related Injures: Evidence for the Prevention Paradox. Annals of Family Medicine www.annfammed.org Vol. 3, No. 1 January/February 2005